DINOSAUR FACT DIG

BRACHIOSAURUS
AND OTHER LONG-NECKED DINOSAURS

THE NEED-TO-KNOW FACTS

BY
REBECCA RISSMAN

Consultant: Mathew J. Wedel, PhD
Associate Professor
Western University of Health Services

CAPSTONE PRESS
a capstone imprint

A+ Books are published by Capstone Press,
1710 Roe Crest Drive, North Mankato, Minnesota 56003
www.mycapstone.com

Library of Congress Cataloging-in-Publication Data
Rissman, Rebecca, author.
Brachiosaurus and other long-necked dinosaurs : the need-to-know facts / by
Rebecca Rissman.
pages cm. – (A+ books. Dinosaur fact dig)
Audience: Ages 4–8.
Audience: K to grade 3.
Summary: "Full-color images and simple text introduce young readers to different
long-necked dinosaurs, including their physical characteristics, habitats, and diets"– Provided
by publisher.
Includes bibliographical references and index.
ISBN 978-1-4914-9647-3 (library binding)
ISBN 978-1-4914-9654-1 (paperback)
ISBN 978-1-4914-9660-2 (eBook PDF)
1. Brachiosaurus–Juvenile literature. 2. Saurischia–Juvenile literature. 3. Dinosaurs–Juvenile
literature. I. Title.
QE862.S3R5535 2016
567.913–dc23   2015028518

EDITORIAL CREDITS:
Michelle Hasselius, editor; Kazuko Collins, designer; Wanda Winch, media researcher;
Gene Bentdahl, production specialist

IMAGE CREDITS: All images by Jon Hughes except: MapArt (maps), Shutterstock: Elena
Elisseeva, green gingko leaf, Jiang Hongyan, yellow gingko leaf, Taigi, paper background

Printed in US.
007535CGS16

**NOTE TO PARENTS, TEACHERS,
AND LIBRARIANS:**
This Dinosaur Fact Dig book uses
full-color images and a nonfiction format
to introduce the concept of long-necked
dinosaurs. *Brachiosaurus and Other
Long-Necked Dinosaurs* is designed to be
read aloud to a pre-reader or to be read
independently by an early reader. Images
help listeners and early readers understand
the text and concepts discussed. The book
encourages further learning by including
the following sections: Table of Contents,
Glossary, Read More, Internet Sites, Critical
Thinking Using the Common Core, and
Index. Early readers may need assistance
using these features.

TABLE OF CONTENTS

WAS THAT AN EARTHQUAKE?

No! That's the booming sound of Brachiosaurus and other long-necked dinosaurs walking. These plant-eating giants lived between 210 and 65 million years ago. They roamed in forests, plains, and coastal areas. Learn more about Brachiosaurus and other enormous dinosaurs, such as Argentinosaurus, Cetiosauriscus, and Rhoetosaurus.

AGUSTINIA

PRONOUNCED: AG-us-TIN-ee-a

NAME MEANING: named after Agustin Martinelli, who found the first Agustinia fossils

TIME PERIOD LIVED: Early Cretaceous Period, 115 to 100 million years ago

LENGTH: 50 feet (15 meters)

WEIGHT: 8.8 tons (8 metric tons)

TYPE OF EATER: herbivore

PHYSICAL FEATURES: long neck and tail, thick body

AGUSTINIA lived alongside other long-necked herbivores, such as Limaysaurus.

Only a few AGUSTINIA bones have been discovered.

Agustinia lived in the forests of what is now Argentina.

N
W　　E
S

where this
dinosaur
lived

Paleontologists first thought **AGUSTINIA** had long, spiny plates on its back. But these bones were from another part of the dinosaur's body.

APATOSAURUS

PRONOUNCED: a-PAT-uh-SAWR-us

NAME MEANING: deceptive reptile, because fossils look like bones from Mosasaur, an ancient water reptile

TIME PERIOD LIVED: Late Jurassic Period, about 150 million years ago

LENGTH: 85 feet (26 m)

WEIGHT: 35 tons (32 metric tons)

TYPE OF EATER: herbivore

PHYSICAL FEATURES: long neck and tail

APATOSAURUS had the widest neck of any dinosaur.

Paleontologists do not think **APATOSAURUS** lived in herds. The dinosaur's fossils are often found alone.

Apatosaurus lived in North America.

N
W E
S

where this
dinosaur lived

APATOSAURUS swallowed
its food whole.

ARGENTINOSAURUS

PRONOUNCED: ARE-jen-TEEN-oh-SAWR-us

NAME MEANING: Argentina lizard

TIME PERIOD LIVED: middle Cretaceous Period, about 100 million years ago

LENGTH: 100 feet (30 m)

WEIGHT: 82 tons (74 metric tons)

TYPE OF EATER: herbivore

PHYSICAL FEATURES: one of the largest dinosaurs that ever lived, legs as large as tree trunks

ARGENTINOSAURUS' eggs were the size of footballs.

Argentinosaurus lived in the forests and plains of what is now Argentina.

N
W ← ◆ → E
S

■ where this dinosaur lived

It took 40 years for **ARGENTINOSAURUS** to reach full size.

ARGENTINOSAURUS had the longest legs of any known dinosaur. Its thighbones were 8 feet (2.5 m) long.

BRACHIOSAURUS

PRONOUNCED: BRACK-ee-uh-SAWR-us

NAME MEANING: arm lizard

TIME PERIOD LIVED: Late Jurassic Period, about 150 million years ago

LENGTH: 85 feet (26 m)

WEIGHT: 25 tons (23 metric tons)

TYPE OF EATER: herbivore

PHYSICAL FEATURES: long neck, small feet for its size

BRACHIOSAURUS ate ferns and tree leaves all day.

BRACHIOSAURUS had a longer neck and shorter tail than most other long-necked dinosaurs.

Brachiosaurus lived in North America.

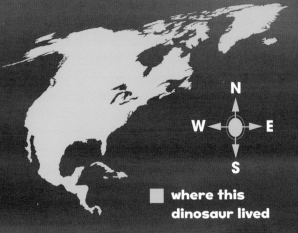

N
W E
S

■ where this dinosaur lived

The dinosaur's ribs were more than 7 feet (2.1 m) long.

BRACHYTRACHELOPAN

PRONOUNCED: BRACK-i-tratch-eh-LOW-pan

NAME MEANING: short-neck shepherd god; fossils were discovered by a shepherd named Daniel Mesa

TIME PERIOD LIVED: Late Jurassic Period, about 150 million years ago

LENGTH: 35 feet (11 m)

WEIGHT: 5.5 tons (5 metric tons)

TYPE OF EATER: herbivore

PHYSICAL FEATURES: long tail, small head, and short neck

BRACHYTRACHELOPAN could not reach tall trees. The dinosaur ate low-growing plants on the ground.

Brachytrachelopan lived in what is now Argentina.

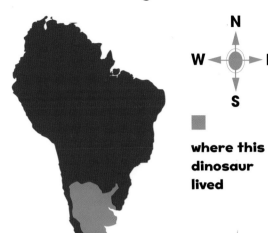

N
W E
S

where this dinosaur lived

BRACHYTRACHELOPAN may have swung its tail like a whip to protect itself from predators.

BRACHYTRACHELOPAN was one of the smallest sauropods.

CAMARASAURUS

PRONOUNCED: KAM-uh-ruh-SAWR-us

NAME MEANING: chambered lizard

TIME PERIOD LIVED: Late Jurassic Period, about 150 to 145 million years ago

LENGTH: 50 feet (15 m)

WEIGHT: 16.5 tons (15 metric tons)

TYPE OF EATER: herbivore

PHYSICAL FEATURES: long neck and tail, small head

CAMARASAURUS is named for the air-filled spaces in its backbone.

A young **CAMARASAURUS** skeleton is one of the most complete dinosaur skeletons ever found. It was discovered in 1925.

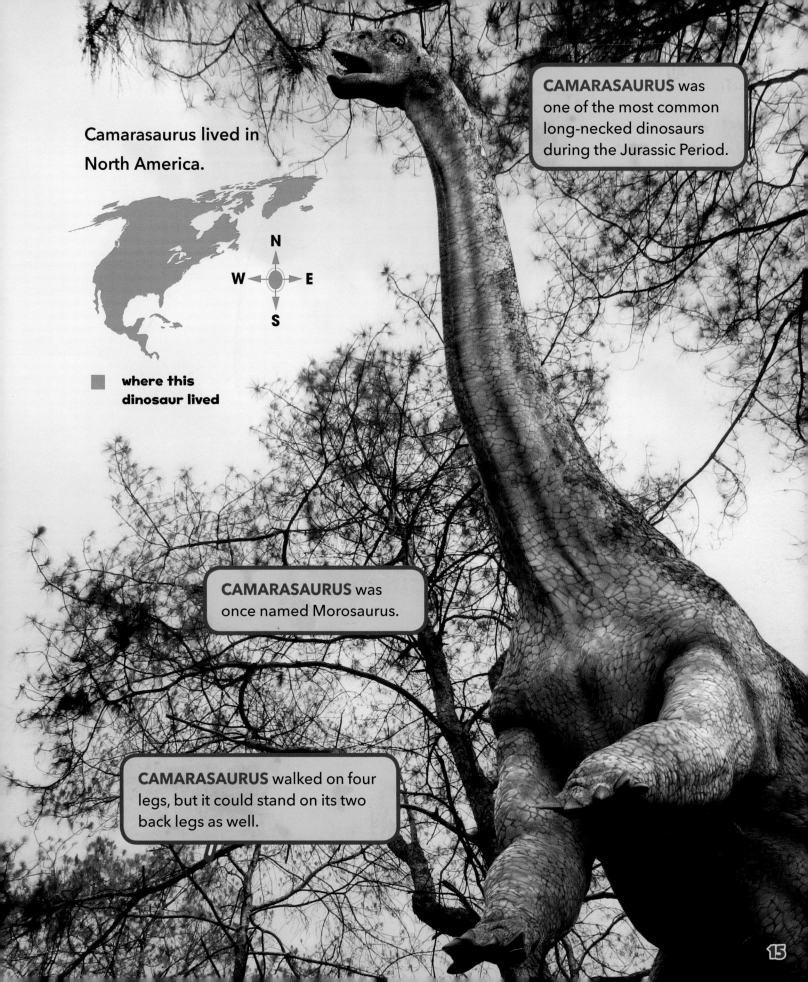

Camarasaurus lived in North America.

N
W ←→ E
S

where this dinosaur lived

CAMARASAURUS was one of the most common long-necked dinosaurs during the Jurassic Period.

CAMARASAURUS was once named Morosaurus.

CAMARASAURUS walked on four legs, but it could stand on its two back legs as well.

CETIOSAURISCUS

PRONOUNCED: SEE-tee-uh-sawr-ISS-kus

NAME MEANING: like whale lizard

TIME PERIOD LIVED: Middle Jurassic Period, about 175 to 160 million years ago

LENGTH: 50 feet (15 m)

WEIGHT: 4.4 tons (4 metric tons)

TYPE OF EATER: herbivore

PHYSICAL FEATURES: strong legs, small head, and long tail

CETIOSAURISCUS had pencil-shaped teeth that pulled leaves off trees.

CETIOSAURISCUS was less than half the length of the longest dinosaurs.

Cetiosauriscus lived in the forests of what is now England.

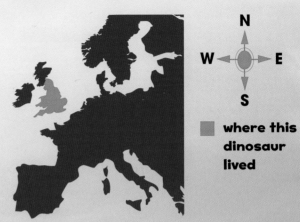

CETIOSAURISCUS whipped its tail from side to side to protect itself from predators.

Only two CETIOSAURISCUS skeletons have ever been found.

DIPLODOCUS

PRONOUNCED: di-PLO-duh-kus

NAME MEANING: double-beamed

TIME PERIOD LIVED: Late Jurassic Period, about 150 million years ago

LENGTH: 90 feet (27 m)

WEIGHT: 12 to 15 tons (11 to 14 metric tons)

TYPE OF EATER: herbivore

PHYSICAL FEATURES: row of small, pointed scales on its back

DIPLODOCUS ate leaves from plants near the ground. It swallowed the leaves whole.

Diplodocus lived in North America.

N
W E
S

where this dinosaur lived

DIPLODOCUS was named after the double-beamed shape of its tailbones.

DIPLODOCUS was long but didn't weigh much more than a large elephant.

HUABEISAURUS

PRONOUNCED: HOO-ah-bay-SAWR-us

NAME MEANING: north China lizard, because fossils were discovered in northern China

TIME PERIOD LIVED: Late Cretaceous Period, about 75 million years ago

LENGTH: 55 feet (17 m)

WEIGHT: 9.4 tons (8.5 metric tons)

TYPE OF EATER: herbivore

PHYSICAL FEATURES: very long neck and tail, large body, and small head

HUABEISAURUS fossils were discovered in 2000.

Like many large dinosaurs, **HUABEISAURUS** had to eat all day. It needed a lot of food to keep its huge body moving.

Huabeisaurus lived in what is now China.

where this dinosaur lived

N
W — S

Paleontologists believe the only **HUABEISAURUS** fossils that have been found are from a young dinosaur. They think an adult could have been even bigger.

OMEISAURUS

PRONOUNCED: OH-mee-SAWR-us

NAME MEANING: Omei lizard, because fossils were found at Omei Shan Mountain in China

TIME PERIOD LIVED: Late Jurassic Period, about 169 to 159 million years ago

LENGTH: 50 to 60 feet (15 to 18 m)

WEIGHT: 5.5 to 9.4 tons (5 to 8.5 metric tons)

TYPE OF EATER: herbivore

PHYSICAL FEATURES: strong and sturdy legs, long neck and tail

OMEISAURUS had 17 bones in its neck. Today's giraffes have seven neck bones.

Many OMEISAURUS fossils were found in the 1970s and 1980s.

Omeisaurus lived what is now China.

where this dinosaur lived

OMEISAURUS stood on its back legs to reach leaves on high branches.

RHOETOSAURUS

PRONOUNCED: ROH-tuh-SAWR-us

NAME MEANING: Rhoetos lizard; Rhoetos was a mythical Greek giant

TIME PERIOD LIVED: Middle Jurassic Period, about 165 million years ago

LENGTH: 55 feet (17 m)

WEIGHT: 22 tons (20 metric tons)

TYPE OF EATER: herbivore

PHYSICAL FEATURES: long tail and strong legs

A complete **RHOETOSAURUS** skeleton has never been found.

Rhoetosaurus lived in what is now Australia.

N

W E

S

where this dinosaur lived

People first thought **RHOETOSAURUS** bones were from a circus elephant.

RHOETOSAURUS could walk about 9 miles (15 kilometers) per hour.

SALTASAURUS

PRONOUNCED: SAWL-tuh-SAWR-us

NAME MEANING: lizard from Salta; fossils were discovered in Salta, Argentina

TIME PERIOD LIVED: Late Cretaceous Period, about 70 to 65 million years ago

LENGTH: 25 feet (8 m)

WEIGHT: 2.2 tons (2 metric tons)

TYPE OF EATER: herbivore

PHYSICAL FEATURES: wide body, plates shaped like spikes along its back

SALTASAURUS was the first armored long-necked dinosaur to be discovered.

Saltasaurus lived in what is now Argentina.

N
W · E
S

■ where this dinosaur lived

SALTASAURUS' neck bones are shaped like an owl's neck bones.

SALTASAURUS was about one-third the size of most long-necked dinosaurs.

SUUWASSEA

PRONOUNCED: SOO-wuss-SEE-uh

NAME MEANING: ancient thunder

TIME PERIOD LIVED: Late Jurassic Period, about 151 million years ago

LENGTH: 50 feet (15 m)

WEIGHT: 11 tons (10 metric tons)

TYPE OF EATER: herbivore

PHYSICAL FEATURES: strong legs, small head, and a short tail

SUUWASSEA had tall backbones. These bones might have formed a hump or short sail on the dinosaur's back.

SUUWASSEA fossils were found on the Native American Crow tribe's territory.

Suuwassea lived in what is now the United States.

where this dinosaur lived

SUUWASSEA lived and traveled in herds to stay safe from predators.

SUUWASSEA was small compared to other long-necked dinosaurs.

GLOSSARY

ANCIENT (AYN-shunt)—from a long time ago

ARMOR (AR-mur)—bones, scales, and skin that some animals have on their bodies for protection

CRETACEOUS PERIOD (krah-TAY-shus PIHR-ee-uhd)—the third period of the Mesozoic Era; the Cretaceous Period was from 145 to 65 million years ago

FERN (FUHRN)—a plant with feathery leaves and no flowers; ferns usually grow in damp places

FOSSIL (FOSS-uhl)—the remains of an animal or plant from millions of years ago that have turned to rock

HERBIVORE (HUR-buh-vor)—an animal that eats only plants

HERD (HURD)—a group of the same kind of animal that live and travel together

JURASSIC PERIOD (ju-RASS-ik PIHR-ee-uhd)—the second period of the Mesozoic Era, the Jurassic Period was from 200 to 145 million years ago

PALEONTOLOGIST (pale-ee-uhn-TOL-uh-jist)—a scientist who studies fossils

PLAIN (PLANE)—a large, flat area of land with few trees

PLATE (PLAYT)—a flat, bony growth

PREDATOR (PRED-uh-tur)—an animal that hunts other animals for food

PRONOUNCE (proh-NOUNSS)—to say a word in a certain way

SCALE (SKALE)—a small piece of hard skin

SPIKE (SPIKE)—a sharp, pointy object; many dinosaurs used bony spikes to defend themselves

CRITICAL THINKING USING THE COMMON CORE

1. Agustin Martinelli discovered the first Agustinia fossils. What is a fossil? (Craft and Structure)

2. Why did Brachytrachelopan eat low-growing plants? (Key Ideas and Details)

3. What was the name of the first armored long-necked dinosaur to be discovered? (Key Ideas and Details)

READ MORE

Matthews, Rupert. *World's Biggest Dinosaurs.* Extreme Dinosaurs. Chicago: Heinemann Library, 2012.

Silverman, Buffy. *Can You Tell a Brachiosaurus from an Apatosaurus?* Dinosaur Look-Alikes. Minneapolis: Lerner Publications Company, 2014.

Wilsdon, Christina. *Wonderful World of Dinosaurs.* Disney Learning. New York: Disney Press, 2012.

INTERNET SITES

FactHound offers a safe, fun way to find Internet sites related to this book. All of the sites on FactHound have been researched by our staff.

Here's all you do:

Visit *www.facthound.com*

Type in this code: 9781491496473

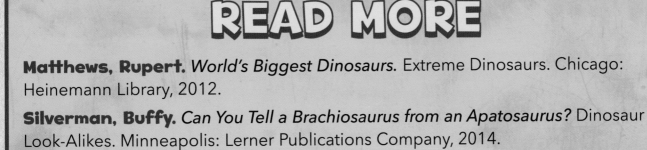

Super-cool stuff!

Check out projects, games and lots more at
www.capstonekids.com

INDEX